Discipleship

as Political Responsibility

Herald Press Titles
by John Howard Yoder

The Christian Witness to the State, 1964, 2002
Discipleship as Political Responsibility, 1964, 2003
*The Original Revolution: Essays on
    Christian Pacifism,* 1971
*Nevertheless: The Varieties and Shortcomings of
    Religious Pacifism,* 1971, 1992
The Legacy of Michael Sattler, Editor and
    Translator, 1973
The Schleitheim Confession, Editor and
    Translator, 1977
What Would You Do? Editor, 1983, 1992
He Came Preaching Peace, 1985
A Declaration on Peace, with Douglas Gwyn,
    George Hunsinger, and Eugene F. Roop, 1991
*Body Politics: Five Practices of the Christian
    Community Before the Watching World,*
    1992, 2001
The Royal Priesthood, 1994, 1998

Discipleship

as Political Responsibility

John Howard Yoder

Translated by Timothy J. Geddert

Herald
Press

Scottdale, Pennsylvania
Waterloo, Ontario

Library of Congress Cataloging-in-Publication Data
Yoder, John Howard.
   [Nachfolge Christi als Gestalt politischer Verantwortung. English]
   Discipleship as political responsibility / John Howard Yoder.
      p. cm.
Includes bibliographical references.
   ISBN 0-8361-9255-9 (pbk. : alk. paper)
1. Christianity and politics. 2. Church and state. 3. Christian life. I. Title.
BR115.P7Y6413 2003
261.7—dc22

                                                           2003015551

Discipleship as Political Responsibility was first published as
Nachfolge Christi als Gestalt politischer Verantwortung (Following
Christ as a Form of Political Responsibility) by Agape Verlag, Basel,
Switzerland in 1964. A second revised edition was published by Agape
Verlag, Weisenheim am Berg, in 2000, ISBN 3-88744-005-6. The
English translation is exclusively available from Herald Press.

Unless otherwise noted, Scripture is from the *Revised Standard Version
Bible*, copyright 1973 by the Division of Christian Education of the
National Council of the Churches of Christ in the USA, and is used by
permission.

DISCIPLESHIP AS POLITICAL RESPONSIBILITY
Copyright © 2003 by Herald Press
Published by Herald Press, Scottdale, Pa. 15683
      Released simultaneously in Canada by Herald Press,
      Waterloo, Ont. N2L 6H7. All rights reserved
Library of Congress Control Number: 2003015551
International Standard Book Number: 0-8361-9255-9
Printed in the United States of America

Front cover: *Vicit agnus noster, eum sequamur.* Medieval print of the
suffering Eucharistic Lamb. Design by Gwen M. Stamm.

10 09 08 07 06 05 04 03   10 9 8 7 6 5 4 3 2 1

To order or request information, please call
1-800-759-4447 (individuals); 1-800-245-7894 (trade).
Website: www.heraldpress.com

Contents

Foreword
to English Edition

"God knows," is often used as a slang expression to express bewilderment when we are faced with the inexplicable. Indeed, "God knows" how to account for the life and work of John Howard Yoder!

I believe the only way we can account for John Howard Yoder is to believe, as he believed, that God never abandons God's creation. Of course, we can try to account for Yoder by filling in his Mennonite background, his education in Europe, the influence of Barth, and Yoder's extraordinary mental power, but all attempts to explain him flounder. We cannot explain Yoder. To come to terms with Yoder means we must be willing to have the presumptions that shape our attempts to explain called into question. How do we explain a miracle?

Miracle is the word Karl Barth used to describe Dietrich Bonhoeffer's dissertation, "Sanctorum Communio: A Theological Study of the Sociology of the Church." Barth's wonderful sense of humor is no doubt behind his use of the word *miracle* to describe Bonhoeffer's work. From Barth's perspective, how else can we explain that such a work could be written in the very heart of Protestant liberalism, the University of Berlin, a university built on the presumption that the language of miracle was the enemy of rational discourse. By describing Bonhoeffer's dissertation as a miracle, Barth was making the serious theological claim that there is no explaining a life or a work like Bonhoeffer's if the God who makes such a life and work possible does not exist. That is what I mean, moreover, by calling Yoder's life and work a miracle.

For this reason, we must be thankful to Herald Press for publishing *Discipleship as Political Responsibility*. These lectures, originally given in German, are an invaluable resource for helping us understand Yoder's challenge to Mennonite and non-Mennonite alike. Some may wonder why we need these lectures just to the extent they represent the initial stages of the position Yoder develops more fully in *The Christian Witness to the State*. It is my belief, however, that these lectures are invaluable for all attempts to provide a scholarly account of Yoder's development. But more important, we need all the Yoder we can get because his work challenges the intellectual habits that make it so difficult to receive his work.

Anyone who understands Yoder must read and reread his texts. I often observe that most of us at our best may from time to time utter an intelligible sentence. Yoder, like MacIntyre and Foucault, spoke in intelligible paragraphs. Moreover, as *Discipleship* makes clear, he could speak in intelligible paragraphs in German or English. His mental powers were extraordinary; but more important was what he had to say. For those of us who would follow after Yoder, we must allow ourselves to be retrained by the speech habits exhibited by his paragraphs. That is why it is important that works like *Discipleship* are made available.

For example, in these lectures Yoder makes the astounding claim that "the ultimate justification for the mandate of the state is to be found within the mandate of the church." Yoder could have learned this from Barth; but I suspect that Barth only confirmed what Yoder had already come to think as he thought through the practices that made his Anabaptist forebears so unusual. Such a claim makes clear that

Anabaptists are anything but "sectarians," because they assume they know what the state—or, "the governing authorities"—are to do better than those authorities can know on their own. Ironically this puts the Anabaptists in the same vicinity as Rome. Like Rome, Anabaptists assume that the functions of the state exist to make the mission of the church possible. Unlike Rome, however, the Anabaptists do not think that normally their task is to assume the office of the governing authorities.

However, as Yoder observes in these lectures, the "state" in our time has acquired a broader meaning than the "sword-function." Accordingly, it may be possible that Christians committed to nonviolence can be called to work for the state. However, they must do so being ever vigilant that the "welfare functions" they perform can be used by the governing authorities to "support the population policy of a totalitarian state." Particularly important in this respect is that Christians not be mesmerized by the language of "democracy." As Yoder reminds us, the difference between democracy and other forms of statehood is a relative difference.

I call attention to Yoder's account of the priority of the church to the governing authorities because I think the radical implications are not easily absorbed. It takes time to receive what John Howard Yoder has to teach us. That is why we must patiently read and reread him. Reading and rereading are required because Yoder forces us to think differently by retraining the very way we speak and write. Accordingly we need all the Yoder we can get. This is why it is so important that we now have *Discipleship as Political Responsibility*.

Stanley Hauerwas
Gilbert T. Rowe Professor of Theological Ethics
Duke University

Foreword

to German Edition, 2000

For decades it has been considered appropriate in discussions about the ethic of peacemaking to challenge people to learn from the historic peace churches. Well-meaning contemporaries can discover with a little effort who the historic peace churches are: the Mennonite Churches which developed out of the nonviolent wing of the Anabaptist movement (sixteenth century); the Quaker movement (seventeenth century); and the Church of the Brethren (eighteenth century). The next step is to become acquainted with the literary sources. That is easier said than done! It is to the merit of Agape Verlag that the theological thinking and piety of the Anabaptist-Mennonite church family has been opened up to a larger public.

This book represents one of the essential documents in this connection, though not available for decades. John Howard Yoder came to Europe after the Second World War as a young volunteer. He worked as an aide in a children's home in Alsace. He completed his doctorate under Karl Barth and because of his incomparably clear and sharp thinking he quickly became one of the most sought after speakers at countless seminars, where he worked for the Anabaptist renewal of his church. In this context he succeeded in reopening the theological debate with the larger church to which persecution had put an end 400 years earlier.

Later, while he was professor at the leading North American peace church seminary, Associated Mennonite Biblical Seminary, he returned often to Europe to promote the "state church—peace church" dialogue. At innumerable ecumenical gatherings he was a speaker and consultant representing peace churches. It is also the result of his tireless efforts that this exchange of ideas was not reduced to the level of mere abstract thought, but rather took into account the full reality of the church's existence, both as a religious fellowship and as an international service fellowship. The very existence of the peace church represents a real alternative to the devilish compulsion to join the murderous pattern of individualistic scapegoating and the collective security policy of our state system.

The present material represents not only a polemic in a larger inter-confessional dispute. It is also a contribution to inter-Mennonite discussion and thus a challenge to Yoder's own church as well. This is why Yoder sometimes refers to "we Mennonites." This also explains why certain things which are taken to be self-evident in a Mennonite milieu, such as the authority of the Bible (with the Sermon on the Mount as the hermeneutical key) and responsible church membership of those baptized as adults, are not discussed, but rather assumed.

Another hurdle results from the fact that so much time has passed since the appearance of the first edition. The theologians and their writings quoted or referred to here will no doubt be familiar to few of the present readers. The scientific study of New Testament times has progressed in the meantime. Key sociological terms that we now take for granted, such as "society" or "the public" do not appear,[*] and thus the important distinction we make today between formal state action and non-governmental activity is also absent. Political entities that do not use violent means, such as the many forms of "active nonviolence" and political mediation, had

[*] Translator's note: Here the author refers to Yoder's non-use of the German terms "Gesellschaft" and "Öffentlichkeit."

not yet appeared. A situation such as the present one in Germany, where one third of those called to military service refuse active participation, was at that time unimaginable.

The ecumenical "Conciliar process for justice, peace and the preservation of creation"—which has perhaps not penetrated the whole church, but has certainly affected many initiatives, groups and service organizations, including many gatherings, pilgrimages, consultations and publications—had not yet come into being. Of even greater influence probably is the fact that those of us living in the age of computers and globalization, those of us who have a decidedly dark ecological prognosis, have a much harder time imagining ourselves to be "Christians in a Constantinian Age" than Yoder here assumes. Today we can only speak of a Christian majority in certain areas, and then only theoretically.

Nevertheless, Yoder's analysis here is relevant, for very often the social and ethical perspectives one finds in churches are still very much influenced by the assumptions of "Constantinian" thought.

At any rate, this text will be of great help to us. There was a school of thought that anticipated when the east-west conflict ended, the threat of war also ended. More realistic analysts anticipated—among other reasons by observing international weapons trading—an increasing number of military confrontations below the level of international atomic war. The Gulf War, the wars in the former Yugoslavia, in both eastern and western Africa and many other places have demonstrated the horrible accuracy of this second prediction. In this situation there have been some attempts—though far too few!—by churches and other Christian groups, to respond with active peacemaking and verbal witness in a way that credibly represents their message of reconciliation.

A far more widely represented posture, however, was one that called for state's use of force as the only instrument strong enough to control the chaos. In evaluating the extent to which this is consistent with or inconsistent with the biblical message, one could have wished that everyone would have remembered the viewpoints of John Howard Yoder. One could have derived from this book the perspectives needed to make such judgments, despite the forty year gap since it was written.

Precisely what Jesus Christ's "peace-church-alternative" looks like in its specifics and how it unfolds in practical situations is not what this book is about. It is rather about the basics. It is fully in line with the author's intentions to view his book as an invitation to ongoing and deeper study of the sort of practical questions that Andrea Lange's book by the same publisher, "Die Gestalt der Friedenskirche" [The Form of the Peace Church], (Weisenheim, 1988) can prepare the reader to pursue. There is a growing body of readily available literature about the reality of the church's "peace-ministry." For those seeking concrete expressions of the peace church alternative, suggestions coming from another branch of the peace church movement, that of the Quakers, will certainly provide helpful insights as well.

May there be many today who accept Yoder's challenging invitation to begin an exploratory journey that leads to Jesus Christ's peace church. May this book breathe new life into the dialogue concerning the peace witness of the church.

—*Wilfried Warneck*

Wilfried Warneck has been manager of the European Peace Church Center "Church and Peace." He was born in Königsberg (Russia) in 1929, he studied Protestant theology and served in a pastoral ministry at a church in Heidelberg. Since 1975, he helped found the ecumenical community "Laurentius-konvent" which has commissioned him for involvement in various peace and development ministries.

Acknowledgment
from First Edition, 1964

Both of the essays in this book originated in 1957. The first, concerning the state in the New Testament, was presented at the Thomashof Bible Center (near Karlsruhe, Germany) on March 17, 1957, at a convention of the International Mennonite Peace Committee. The second, concerning following Christ as a form of political responsibility, was delivered in Iserlohn (Germany) on July 29, 1957, as the opening address at a theological conference convened for the sake of dialogue between representatives of the German State Church and representatives of the so-called "Historic Peace Churches" (the second Puidoux-Conference). *—The Publishers*

— I —

The State in the New Testament

What is unique about the problem we are addressing here is that it is not solved by interpreting the New Testament; in fact interpreting the New Testament creates the problem! The big question is not, "What does the New Testament say about the state?" but rather, "What do we do with that which the New Testament says?" After all, the state we know today is not like the state spoken of in the New Testament. Christians in the New Testament were a small, persecuted minority under the control of the Roman Empire. Jesus was a Jew under foreign occupation. In these respects our situation today is completely different.

If we want to learn from the Bible, therefore, we are confronted with two questions. First, what does the Bible say? Second, how are we to apply what the Bible says? It is best to keep these questions completely separate, since they are questions of two different sorts. If we mix them we will not provide an appropriate answer to either.

The first question is a question of objective fact: What does the Bible teach? The second asks to what degree we want to allow the Bible's teaching to be valid for us today. We will therefore proceed as follows: In four thesis statements, we will investigate how "state" is understood in the thought world of the New

Testament. In this part we will not pose questions relating to the application of New Testament perspectives in the present world. After that we will expand the inquiry, asking whether and how the biblical teaching should apply today, that is, how and where we can build bridges from the early church[1] to the present.

The Mandate of the State

The divine mandate of the state consists in using evil means to keep evil from getting out of hand.

It would be perfectly natural if human violence and selfishness destroyed human society. Humans are so constituted, and their sinfulness stands in such stark conflict with the ground of their own existence that humanity could very quickly destroy itself. And yet, what one would expect to happen to sinful humanity does not happen, for God has mandated that the state uphold a measure of order. What is peculiar to this "relative order" is that evil is applied to itself, so to speak. People protect themselves—motivated by selfishness and using violence —against the violence and the selfishness of other people. This does not mean that God considers either the violence or the selfishness to be a good thing, or that God wills them. God wants humans to be neither violent nor selfish. However, since humanity has fallen away from God, God permits human evil to keep itself under control by using evil against itself.

Even the life of Cain, the first murderer, was put under a sign of protection. That means that the law of retribution, evil for evil, a life for a life, was established to keep Cain alive (Gen. 4:15). In the covenant with Noah this law was expanded to protect all of humanity (Gen. 9:5). This order of the sword that has ruled humanity from earliest times is not God's form of justice or redemption; nevertheless it represents an expression of God's grace aimed at redemption, by keeping God's fallen creation in existence (however destructive sin itself is) with a view toward the God-intended redemption of the fallen creation. The classic New Testament texts that deal with this topic (Rom. 13 and 1 Pet. 2) say exactly what we find in the first pages of the Bible. (And here we need to be reminded that we are talking about the order of the sword. The New Testament does not deal with the state in terms of its role in funding school systems, building roads, administering social programs, regulating postal services, and all the other things that we also think of today when referring to the "state.")

It is important to note in which contexts and with which sorts of expressions the New Testament could come to view the state as a tool in God's hand. It does not come in a discussion of creation or nature in which there is a principle of order intended by God and in which the state also has its place. According to the New Testament, the place where the agency of the sword belongs is a different one. The Old Testament text that most frequently appears in the New Testament is not Isaiah 53; it is not the Ten Commandments; it is not the Love Command. It is Psalm 110: "The Lord says to my lord: 'Sit at my right hand, till I make your enemies your footstool.'" This verse which no longer has any special place in our contemporary piety was of central importance to the early church, and we must begin with it if we are to understand how the early church thought about the state.

This Psalm speaks of the "enemies" of the Messiah. The New Testament identifies these enemies with the "powers, rulers, principalities, thrones." In today's world it is not easy to understand what was meant by these terms. But certainly we will be able to understand the New Testament only if we adopt the New Testament's thought patterns and understand these terms to refer to concrete powers. Such powers had responded to Christ with hostility, but Jesus became Lord through his death, resurrection and ascension; his Lordship extends even over these powers, who, as a result, will have to bend their knees (Phil. 2:10). Of these Christ made a spectacle, just as a returning victor does in a triumph march (Col. 2:15).

Among these powers—that is those at enmity with Christ, those fallen powers that became subject to Christ —the early Christians included the state. The early church respected the state and made room for the state, yet they did not do so because they viewed it as part of God's good creation. On the contrary, they viewed it as part of the world that opposes God, that is already defeated by Christ in principle, and over which the exalted Christ already rules until he has defeated his last enemy (1 Cor. 15:25ff.).

From this perspective we can better understand the mood of the early church as it looked the Roman state in the face and made room for it, but defied its persecution. They viewed it as one of God's defeated enemies. The Christians saw in the state's demonic self-worship (Rev. 14:14ff.) evidence that its glory days were numbered. For precisely this reason they could concede to the state that arena in which it was still temporarily allowed to forestall violence by means of violence (Rom. 13). We grossly misunderstand the "divine ordering of the state" if we forget that we are talking here about the pagan state.[*] It was not David or Josiah, the Elector of Saxon, or the Council of Geneva—those referred to in European Christendom when people defended the state's claim to authority. On the contrary, the apostle is referring to the pagan Caesar when he writes: "There is no authority except from God." How God can use that which is pagan, indeed that which is demonic, without affirming it, is something that human understanding cannot completely grasp. But that is what the early church believed, and that is what the Scriptures teach.

---

[*] The German word *heidnisch* is translated "pagan" wherever possible; occasionally "non-Christian" seemed to convey better both the meaning and the tone of Yoder's text. In such cases, an asterisk indicates that the underlying German word is the same one usually translated "pagan."

The Mandate of the Church

The divine mandate of the church consists in overcoming evil through the cross.

Praising God is at the very center of the Christian church's mandate. When we gather for worship, when we proclaim the gospel in the world, when we practice acts of love, we are to proclaim the virtues of the one who called us to the light and who made us into the people of God. At this point we must call special attention to the aspect of this mandate that has to do with our relationship to the state and to evil.

The posture of the Christian in relation to evil fits into the category of "following Jesus." This concept has become so familiar, so commonplace, so cheap, that we do not properly understand what following really means. What it means is something completely revolutionary.

The early church believed that God was at work within the church by means of Jesus Christ living on within it. The apostle Paul could say that it was no longer he himself who lived; rather Christ was living in him. He could claim that he could do all things through Christ (Phil. 4:13); he could go even further and claim that in his own flesh he was filling up what was still missing in the suffering of Christ (Col. 1:24). For us these claims, especially the last one, seem strange. To dare to make such audacious claims about one's own faith journey offends our pious sensibilities; it seems repugnant to our modesty, to the humility with which we are accustomed to speaking of faith issues. We would consider it presumptuous if persons were to talk about themselves in this way today, as if that person's life was in some special way bound up with Christ himself.

Yet it is precisely in this seeming presumptuousness that the heart of the Christian faith lies. The early Christians had the audacity to believe quite literally in the Holy Spirit. If it seems too presumptuous to us, if it does not seem humble enough, when Paul speaks without any embarrassment of Christ's work in him, then we should ask ourselves if our humility has not stolen our courage to believe in the Holy Spirit today.

If the church believed such things about itself and testified to their reality, then the church did not view the way of the cross which the church traveled in following Jesus (Mark 10:39; Luke 14:26ff.; John 15:20) as some sort of extra moral achievement, something that would have been optional and commendable, but which they could have done without. They viewed it as something that belongs to the very essence of God's salvation plan for the world. The cross-carrying following which the church practices, that is the continuing life of Jesus through his Spirit in the members of his body, is not an implication, something tacked on; rather it is part of his saving work. That is what the New Testament means when it speaks of following, of the body of Christ, of the Holy Spirit—that God's continuing work today is no less valid, no less divine, no less urgent than it was from the start. Just as God was at work through the person of God's own Son, so God continues to be at work in the church in the form of the Spirit.

It is self-evident, and never to be forgotten, that the cross of the church has no meaning without Jesus. Suffering in itself does not accomplish any saving work. But we are too reluctant to confess the other side along with the Scriptures, namely, that without the cross of the church, the cross of Christ would be emptied.

But the question to be asked now is this: What is the relationship between these two mandates, the mandate of the state and the mandate of the church?

Our answer is found in 1 Timothy 2:1ff., which commands us to pray for the political leaders and for peace, *because God desires everyone to be saved.* Saving people and bringing them to the knowledge of the truth were not achievements of the Roman Empire. This means that the ultimate justification for the mandate of the state is to be found within the mandate of the church. The mandate of the church, the mandate to overcome evil, is the superior mandate; the mandate of the state, that of keeping evil in check, only has meaning because the church is accomplishing its mission. Ephesians 3:10 makes similar claims when it says that the church is to proclaim to the "powers" that God's ultimate purpose is the building of a church. Again the early church dared to be audacious, claiming that the glorious Roman Empire,[*] standing as something unique in world history, existed for one purpose only: that God could use a small, despised bunch of fishermen and tax collectors to carry forth the name of an executed Galilean from Jerusalem into the whole world. We are far too accustomed to this idea. We can hardly imagine how audacious it was back then. But the early Christians did far more than merely believe this crazy idea, this offensive viewpoint; they went on to testify to and demonstrate the truth of their faith by means of their suffering victory march through the world.

State-sponsored religions everywhere have viewed religion as support for the state—an educating, morality-teaching, consecrating power. The Christian faith inverted this relationship and viewed the world-embracing empire as merely a support system, subservient to the real work God is accomplishing in the world.

The Limits of the State

The state is limited by its mandate. The mandate of the state cannot involve an unlimited authority. Part of its very being is to keep not only foreign evil in check, but also itself. Jesus' own words, "'Then render to Caesar the things that are Caesar's, and to God the things that are God's,'" (Luke 20:25) indicate that the state's claims for itself are limited by the

---

[*] Wherever possible the German word *Staat* has been translated "state"; occasionally, as here, "Empire" seemed more appropriate.

unconditional claim of one higher. What belongs to Caesar—the coin with his image—that we can hand over to Caesar. But with this statement Jesus did not bring the matter to a close as he would have had to if he had wanted to speak in support of the state. Rather, without even being asked to do so, he drew his questioners' attention to God's claim on their own lives. No doubt Paul is providing his own commentary on this word of Jesus, when he says, "Pay all of them their dues" (Rom. 13:7). With the list he provides (tax, duty, fear, honor) he is not providing a list of all the things that belong to the state, otherwise he would be speaking nonsense. Rather he is giving a list of things about which we must make decisions in line with the word of Jesus as to whether they belong to Caesar or to God. Again it is made clear that we must always keep in mind the limits of the state. The same is obvious when we note how Romans 13 begins (a text in which the Greek word *taxis*, i.e. order, is frequently used). It also becomes obvious when we note how verse 8 answers the question concerning to whom we are indebted (note how verse 8 directly relates to verse 7!): we have no debt to anyone, except the debt of love.

When we speak of the state we often speak of a "just state," or a "constitutional state," and thus imply that there are limits to the violence a state is permitted to exercise. Even from a Christian perspective, the concept of a "just state" is useful. Now of course the justice of the state is in no way to be equated with God's own justice. God's justice is God's grace. God is just in that God forgives us our sins (1 John 1:9). In terms of a just state, this is not the case. Since God has given the state a mandate which is bound by clear standards, the state has its own kind of justice, or perhaps better, legal mandate, that permits us to call the state to account, using a measurement related to its own mandate. We may, indeed we should, demand of the state, even the non-Christian[*] state, that it be

---

[*] German *heidnisch*.

just. The apostle Paul did not just tell the state authority he was dealing with, "As a Christian I would not be able to be in your position"; he also told him that as an official he should deal correctly, in accordance with the law.

Of course the early Christians had very little opportunity to address the state in terms of its own righteousness. But in principle that was clearly part of the church's testimony, for only the church knew why and for what purpose the state existed. The very fact that the apostle made use of his right as a citizen is proof that the church, though structurally not part of the state, had the right to address the state about its mandate. That was part of the mandate of the church.

When we speak of the boundaries, limits, and justice of the state, we make the assumption that the state can become unjust by overstepping its boundaries. For good reason the New Testament takes this possibility into account. The powers that Jesus made subservient to himself can still rise up in opposition to him. That sort of state is described as a beast out of the abyss (Rev. 13) and as a demonic power. This rebellion of the state can be explicitly religious, as it was when Rome demanded that the Christians confess "Caesar is Lord." The state can also demand or practice injustice in practical matters and thus overstep its boundaries. The church has a mission in relation to this kind of state as well. Here it becomes even more important to make sure that honor and fear are given only to the One to whom it is due. The suffering followership of the church becomes the valid response to an unjust state, "the endurance and the faith of the saints" (Rev. 13:10; 14:12).

The State as a Pagan Institution

The state is a pagan institution in which a Christian would not normally hold a position. The first Christians were not "statesmen," and those who held a political office and became Christians normally gave up their office. One explanation for this is simply the historical situation of the time. At first the Christians were reckoned among the Jews, who were in no way involved in administering the Roman political system. For the most part they were not Roman citizens and that automatically excluded them from most offices. They came primarily from the lower and middle societal levels. They were slaves, traveling merchants and handworkers. Political officials were not normally recruited from such circles. But even more significant than the above was the religious sub-structure of the state itself. The state, that is the Roman Empire, was not a purely technical, spiritually neutral, administrative machine; it was a religion. The Caesar was honored as divine. Both in oaths and in the acclamation that "Caesar is Lord," one consecrated the very being of the state as something divine. This in itself made it impossible for Christians to serve as state officials.

Still it would be an error to assume the posture of the first Christians and of the New Testament in relation to the state was determined solely by social, political, and religious circumstances of the day, and that everything would have been different if the Christians had belonged to the leading classes, or if the state had not had this religious substructure. There are a variety of considerations that speak against this downplay of the contrary position.

The State as a Pagan Institution—Objective Considerations

There is first of all a purely practical consideration. If the very nature of the church is to confront evil with suffering, cross-carrying love, and if the very nature of the state is to confront evil with threat and if necessary with violence against violence, how can a person be involved in both at the same time? Can a person simultaneously pull out the sword and "turn the other cheek"? The New Testament explicitly reckons with the incompatibility of these two functions. Romans 12:19 speaks of the intentional renunciation of "vengeance" on the part of the Christian. Vengeance is God's business. Seven verses later it is stated that God's "instrument of vengeance" is the governing authority. That means the God has taken the vengeance role (the role of violent self-defense) away from the church in order to entrust it to the state. If the church itself were to deal with the injustice done to it, how could the church still proclaim the gospel of forgiveness? (cf. 1 Cor. 6:7: "Why not rather suffer wrong?") Both ministries, that of the church and that of the state, are carried out in accordance with God's will and God's appointment. However, they cannot be carried out simultaneously by the same person; their very nature is too different for that. Where it is necessary to choose between the two, Christians in the New Testament choose the higher calling.

Still it would be wrong to conclude this sort of practical consideration is the only way to demonstrate that the functions of the church and state are irreconcilable. After all, one can be deceived by logical arguments. Even more important are two observations from the Scriptures, which confirm what the practical considerations have suggested. These observations show us that the basic position presented here is not something first discovered by the early Christians. They demonstrate that Jesus and before him the old covenant supported this basic position.

The State as a Pagan Institution—Old Testament

We will turn our attention first to the Old Testament and ask how the people of God were progressively prepared for Jesus Christ. In this matter we do well to start where Israel seems to be farthest away from Christ—both in terms of time and in terms of nature—that is, in the "holy wars" of the premonarchy. These "wars" were totally different than state measures; they were divine miracles. They were proof that

God was to be King over God's people. This does not merely mean that there were no generals; it means there was not
even a state. When an emergency situation threatened Israel,
somebody "blew the trumpet" and immediately the country-
people flooded together, without proper weapons, in no rea-
sonable power relation to the enemy power, and God gave
them the victory. It happened without the help of the state.
The trumpet parade around Jericho and Gideon's three hun-
dred men armed with clay pots cannot be viewed as powers
of the state. These wars were not military battles; in the
deepest sense of the word they were experiences of divine
worship. In many respects it is impossible for these wars to
be valid models for us in the New Covenant, since by God's
grace we understand God's will more clearly. Still, they do
capture this truth: In the early days when Israel still had no
king, it was God's will that they live without a governing system even in the extreme situation of a war, in order that Israel
would be directly dependent on God's powerful grace.

  As soon as Israel got a king "like the other nations" the
situation changed. Saul began to abandon the odd and unre-
liable customs of earlier times; he aimed to build up a nation
state with a standing army and a reasoned military policy.
For example, he retained the booty instead of destroying it as
a great offering. And from that point on, God called forth
prophets, starting with Samuel in Saul's time, who saw in
these political transactions by Israel's kings the embodiment
of disobedience.

  A typical example of these prophets is Isaiah. He hunted
out King Ahaz "at the upper pool" (Isa. 7), where he was no
doubt examining fortifications in light of a war threat. Ahaz
was not commanded to follow through on defense measures,
but rather to trust in God, for God wanted to be personally
responsible to make sure the calamity would not occur. On
another occasion, (Isa. 18, 30, 31) the prophet depicted God
as the one who would personally appear to save Israel; God

would come in a thunderstorm, would come as a lion, would swoop down as a bird from on high to protect its young. This salvation would be nothing short of miraculous. It would not even be a holy war; it would not require even the trumpets of Joshua or the pitchers of Gideon. But the political officials did not have enough faith to trust God. They had more faith in their alliances with Egypt, and in their horses and chariots. And it proved to be their undoing. Because they despised the "waters of Shiloah that flow gently," the Assyrian flood swept them away (Isa. 8:6-8).

Jeremiah took this critique of the state even further. He recommended capitulating to the enemy (Jer. 27) and warned the captives to set their hopes on a speedy return from their captivity (Jer. 29). It is with regard to the fate of those in captivity that the songs of God's suffering servant (Isa. 42, 49) sound forth their proclamation: God's work in the world requires the willingness of God's own people to surrender their own existence. The suffering of God's people, deprived of all political protection, becomes a prophetic word pointing to Christ (Isa. 53), who was handed over to others in the very same way, innocent and without protection.

The State as a Pagan Institution—New Testament

And with that we come to the New Testament. Does the New Testament even address the question whether a person can serve God according to the methods appropriate for the state and at the same time according to those appropriate for the church? Answer: We do not introduce this question from outside and impose it on the New Testament. On the contrary, this question is very clearly addressed within the New Testament itself—and not in relation to just anyone. It is addressed in relation to the perfect one, Jesus himself. Recent research (see, for example, Oscar Cullmann, *The State in the New Testament*, New York: Scribners, 1956) demonstrates clearly that Jesus was confronted with concrete political problems, a fact which our usual ways of examining the Bible do not bring to light.

The reference here is primarily to the Zealot option. The Zealots (zealous fanatics) were significant players in the political life of the time. In the context of the Roman occupation of Palestine these were the freedom-fighters who wanted to drive pagan rulers out of the land by means of a "holy war" (a term that originally meant something totally different). Their uprisings continued after the time of Jesus and became the occasion for the destruction of Jerusalem. Jesus could not avoid dealing with them. He proclaimed the "Kingdom of God" and that is also what they wanted. One of his twelve disciples (and for all we know others as well) came from among the Zealots. Jesus was close enough to the Zealots that he could win disciples out of their movement. He was close enough that the charge against him, namely that he was a Zealot and pretender to the throne, could be presented as the legal grounds for his execution. He was close enough that it must have been a serious temptation for him to join their program.

Let us just imagine what a tie to the Zealots would have meant for Jesus. He would have been called out as Messiah, and virtually the whole nation would have risen up, granted him the throne, and supported him in driving out the Romans, protected and supported by his miracle-working power. He would have set up a just state; he would have helped God's elect acquire dominion over the whole world as they had been promised. If there was ever a time one would have been justified in assuming the reins of power, this was it.

This is what Jesus' temptations after his baptism were about. Dominion over the world was offered to him. It was suggested that he demonstrate his Messiahship through a bread-miracle or by appearing suddenly from on high in the court of the temple (as a fulfillment of Mal. 3:1). This is also what was involved when people tried to make him king after he performed the bread-miracle (John 6:15). And in the end this is what was involved in Gethsemane, as he considered the possibility that perhaps the cup of suffering might "pass from him." When he renounced the protection of "twelve legions of angels," he resisted one last time the devil's offer. He chose the cross and rejected kingship.

We have a hard time today imagining what this was all about: how he could have fed the multitudes with a bread-miracle; how he might have descended from the roof of the temple into the temple court; what the messianic state would have looked like; how the angels would have fought for him. But this much is clear: according to the New Testament viewpoint, these were real possibilities for Jesus. He had real choices to make about them. There was another way he could have gone; he could have avoided the cross by seizing political power. If he, the perfectly righteous one, could not simultaneously choose these two options, if he chose to leave the political option in the hands of Pilate, if he declined the option of state-sponsored violence in order to choose the cross, this is surely the final proof that the two forms of service are irreconcilable. Even God, in the person of God's Son, cannot combine the two in one person. God intentionally left the state in the hands of pagans; God has other means, more effective means, of working in and for the world.

The stance of Christ and the early church toward the state is open to two objections. These same objections are also voiced today against people who hold Jesus' views. They are, however, not modern objections. They do not concern the application of New Testament teaching; they concern the teaching itself. If these objections are valid, then they are critiques of Jesus and of the New Testament.

The first of these is that if the state is "left to the non-Christians"[*] one is handing it over to the devil and giving up

---

[*] German *Heiden.*

all concern for what happens to things. Would it not be so much better to take control of things than to hand them over to evil people and evil powers? If decent people are not concerned about things, who knows what will eventually result?

This objection loses its force if we join the New Testament in believing that not even the pagan world is so fully autonomous that God has no control over it. As we saw earlier, it is a basic conviction of the New Testament that not only pagans, but even the demonic powers behind the state have already been brought under the lordship of the resurrected one who sits at God's right hand, even though things do not always look this way on the surface. This means that when Jesus and the first Christians left the sword in the hands of the pagan state, they were not handing it over to the devil, but rather to God's ultimate lordship.

The second objection is that Christians who take this stance are irresponsible parasites. They enjoy the protection of the state but refuse to take on the burden of helping to lead it and to do its work. They are happy to draw benefits from the solidarity provided by others, but are unwilling to contribute to that solidarity themselves. This was the objection that the non-Christian Celsus, for example, raised against the Christians. But it loses its force just as quickly as the other objection does if we believe along with the New Testament (as the church father Origen responded to Celsus) that through their Gospel proclamation, their prayers of supplication, their discipleship in the context of suffering, and their service of loving the neighbor, Christians contribute not less, but far more to human solidarity and therefore to the state than the political officials themselves.

The Problem of Application

In the previous points we have established conclusions about the New Testament's perspective on the state. But in doing so we have intentionally avoided making hasty connections between the New Testament teaching and the present; the New Testament needs to be understood first within its own presuppositions. But now we must ask whether there is any way of finding a connection between what the New Testament says and the present.

The majority of theologians and churches are united in their response to this question. Most would concede that the New Testament speaks of the relationship between the church and the world as we have portrayed it. But all of that, they would claim, lays no obligation on us. This is so because *our world* has become in every respect so different from the world of the first century that we do not know what to do with the stance of the New Testament. Today's states are no longer anything like the state of the first century, and the church has changed just as much. As a result, the majority of churches and theologians have concluded that Christians today must go in a completely new direction.

So even if we want to address only the teaching of the New Testament, we have no choice but to address the question of whether that teaching (as sketched above) is normative for us today.

Of course we do not want to deny in any way that a great deal has changed. The acceptance of the church by the emperor Constantine and his interference with its official teaching, the persecution of pagans under Theodosius, the permission given by Augustine that Christians of different persuasions be persecuted, the events of the Middle Ages, of the Reformation, and our own age, which first "Christianized" Europe and then "de-Christianized" it again—all of these have brought about basic changes in the relationship between the church and the world. Even if we wanted to deny this, we could not do so. The question is not whether we are still living in the world of 65 C.E., nor whether the world and the church are still basically the same as back then. The question is whether the many changes that have occurred since then lead us to conclude that the New Testament teaching is not valid for us.

The fact is that the majority of theologians and churches simply ignore this distinction; they assume that by recognizing how much the situation has changed, we have automatically found justification for ignoring the New Testament viewpoint on this matter. It seems as though it has never occurred to them that there is another option, namely that the teaching of the New Testament might still be valid even though the situation has changed. With respect especially to our fourth thesis, in which it was observed that the carrying out of state sanctioned violence is, according to the New Testament, clearly a pagan mandate, the majority opinion is that there is no way to accept this view today.

By claiming that the times have changed, they pursue a hidden agenda, that of looking for other guidelines to replace the scriptural ones. For the Catholicism of the Middle Ages these guidelines were simply the norms of the Roman state, taken over with hardly any modification. For the Reformation it was the absolutely fixed concepts of "government authority" and "calling," and the assumption that these terms were self-evident and equally valid for Christian and non-Christian* alike. In the Age of the Enlightenment it was the terms "Freedom" and "Democracy," and in our day it is all too often the concept that God has chosen a particular nation or race. These solutions have one thing in common: All have been used by Christians to free themselves from biblical guidelines for understanding the relationship between church and world, and in one way or another all have been adopted in order to use non-Christian norms to guide and justify the behavior of Christians.

Since there are so many who adopt this view as "Christian" and "right," we have an obligation to examine

---

* German *Heiden.*

more closely their arguments, and also to make sure we do not merely claim our alternative, but also explain it.

The first question to ask is how we should evaluate the changes in the situation of the church since apostolic times. Secondly, we must look more closely at the various aspects of the changes themselves and ask whether they are sufficient to dismiss the New Testament teaching. Thirdly, we need to ask ourselves how we should think about our relationship to the state today, if the Scriptures are indeed to be a valid guide.

The Problem with Progress

The first thing we must do is ask the basic question: Was it progress when the Roman state became Christian in the fourth century? Most church historians and theologians have viewed it as that, starting with Constantine's contemporary Eusebius and continuing on through the Reformation and for many on up to the present. Lying behind all the changes that have occurred is this one, the first and most important of them all. The way we evaluate this change will not only determine our stance in relation to the state, but also our concept of the church itself. That this change was a very important change is of course a claim with which we agree. But the question is, was it a change for the better, a change that we evaluate positively in our Christian thinking? The Middle Ages and the Reformation claimed that it was.

The first thing to be clear about is that the New Testament contains no expectation of such "progress"; that is, there is no expectation in the New Testament that there would be a basic change, one to be evaluated positively, in the relationship between the church and the world. Of course the state can change its stance on things; the state can follow through on its mandate (Rom. 13) or it can make itself into a false god (Rev. 13); but whichever it does it is still pagan. The New Testament does not reveal an expectation that things will improve. On the contrary, it expects the situation will worsen for the church, resulting in even more serious persecution and many Christians falling from the faith. If we evaluate the "Christianizing of the state" in light of the New Testament's own terms and value judgments, then we should be thinking of the change as "falling away," rather than as "progress."

The birth hour for the Anabaptist movement struck in Zurich in October 1523, when the reformer Ulrich Zwingli handed over the question of whether or not to dispense with the unbiblical practice of the mass to the city council in Zurich. Zwingli could do that only because he, along with the other reformers and with the Middle Ages, believed that those in the city council were not only Christians, but were Christians worthy of special honor who were specially led by God. This is where Simon Stumpf and Conrad Grebel cried out, "Stop!" In their view, the Scriptures alone remain the authority, even for the external life of the church, even if the state calls itself Christian. If the mass is unbiblical, then government officials, even if they are Christians, *especially* if they are Christians, have no right to retain it. At this point, and not at the time of their first baptism, the Anabaptist movement became a concrete historical reality. The right to exist for the Anabaptists did not come about because of their baptismal practices, nor because of the social ethic they adopted, nor because they refused to bear arms or take oaths. The right to exist for the Anabaptists emerged from their basic refusal to accept any authority, even if it claims to be Christian, alongside or above the Bible. The Anabaptists responded with a clear "No" to the idea that the situation can change so much that the New Testament is no longer a valid authority, and to the idea that the state can in fact be Christian. If they were wrong in these basic convictions, then Anabaptism (and also Mennonitism) has no valid reason to exist; after all, every other issue, whether their convictions

about baptism, their understanding of church, disc
or social ethics, or their preference for tolerance, is 1
their posture towards Scripture.

The claim that civilization's progress makes the New
Testament no longer normative has, of course, been made not
only with reference to the problem of the state. Almost any
faith confession in Scripture can be circumvented in a similar way. For example, some argue this: in New Testament
times people believed in miracles. So people could tell sto-
ries about miracles Jesus performed. Now we know that such
things do not happen. As a result we need to bracket the parts
of the Gospel that report such events. Or, as others argue, in
New Testament days people believed that the gods could
appear in human form (Acts 14:11), so the apostles could
describe Jesus as God's Son. Now we know that such ideas
are philosophically impossible. So we need to strike those
parts from the record. This is how people have argued. And
as Christians we agree that in these matters it is not appropriate to "correct" the Bible on the basis of "progress." One
needs to ask why things should be different in terms of the
state.

A half century ago people still believed in the concept of
progress. At that time everything seemed to be moving forward. Education, technical know-how, economic progress—
everything seemed to be progressing. Humanity itself was
thought to be improving. Europe's belief in God had been
rewarded with dominion over the world. Who would doubt
that the whole development of the world to this point, including the Constantinian turn-around and the Reformation, was
God's way of leading things forward and upward? At that
time it seemed natural to affirm the "Christian-ness" of the
state within this larger development—and simultaneously
the necessity of "correcting" the New Testament. However,
by now we have learned a few things in the "Christian West."
We no longer believe that all change is progress. And as a

ıesult, we can no longer believe as easily as we once did, that every step leading to the present critical situation has been a step forward.

The Significance of the Changed Situation in Detail

We have every reason to be skeptical of claims that things have progressed beyond the New Testament. And yet claims that are made need to be examined seriously. What exactly has changed?

1. Instead of being persecuted, the church is recognized and favored by the world. That this change has indeed happened is not to be denied. But this does not affect the basic issue. Even the church in the New Testament experienced times of peace, but that did not mean that the state was evaluated differently or that Christians started moving into governmental positions.

2. The number of Christians has increased to the extent that a large portion, often the majority or the totality, of the population is Christian. Although the minority church of the earliest years was able to leave the state in the hands of others without further ado, that would be impossible today. Today it is not possible, nor would it be desirable, for Christians to keep their distance from the state.

At first glance this argument seems beyond refutation. But in no way is this really so. Let us be clear first that we are playing games with words here. The designation "Christian" does not have the same meaning in the two situations. When we say that in the early church the Christians were in the minority, we are referring to convinced believers, who, however deep or shallow their faith might have been, at least had to be willing to suffer for their convictions. When we speak of the Middle Ages or of the Reformation and say that Christians were in the majority, we are no longer referring to the convinced, but rather to those who were baptized as infants, whether they took a personal faith stance toward their baptism or not. The distinction we are making here is not a sectarian or pietistic one. It is one that derives from Augustine, and later from both Luther and Calvin, who connected to their teaching concerning the invisibility of the true church and predestination the conviction that the truly elect and those Christians with an inner faith were a small minority within the larger visible territorial church. To concede this is to invalidate the entire argument. If the true Christians are really still a minority, why then should the teaching of the New Testament not remain normative?

There is another reason why this argument is not conclusive. It also assumes that the state must always be in the hands of the majority of the population. But this is by no means a necessary assumption. For most of world history this was not the case anywhere, and today it is also not true for much of the world. Even if true Christians made up the majority of the world's population, this would contribute nothing new to the question at hand.

3. Political leaders have themselves become Christians. As the Swiss Reformation theologian Heinrich Bullinger expressed it: "The princes have become the saviors and the nourishers of the church." But this argument also seems convincing only if we persist in keeping the concepts unclear. If a "prince" has become Christian in the sense that he is ready to leave all for Christ's sake and follow him, then the situation of the New Testament still applies. If he has become Christian in the sense that, while belonging to the visible church he retains the freedom to act as a non-Christian[*] in the way he lives out his official position in the state, then the New Testament position concerning the state still applies, only in this case the church has become unfaithful.

4. Since Napoleon it has become commonplace to require military service of everyone. True. But it does not

---

[*] German *heidnisch*.

follow that a military responsibility is a Christian responsibility. At the time of the Roman Empire it was also required across the board that people worship Caesar. Yet Christians did not yield to this requirement. At the time of the Reformation the baptizing of infants was required across the board. But our ancestors did not yield to this requirement. In terms of the state's right to require military service across the board, a serious and questionable change has come about. It changes nothing, however, in terms of the Scripture's view of the state. It only represents an unfavorable change in the state.

5. Today we make a distinction between a totalitarian and a welfare state. The state is not there only to guard our physical security; the state also builds roads, leads schools, provides medical services, cares for the elderly, and delivers everyone's mail. Finally we come in contact with a change that really is a change from New Testament times. (The Roman Empire[*] did in fact have a postal system and certain welfare systems; however, these were not generally available and the New Testament does not deal with this reality.) Many of the activities of the modern state are only remotely connected, or not connected at all with the exercise of violence to protect what is right. Still, even here we are confronted with a difference only in terms of concepts. While it is true that we today understand the word "state" more broadly, the same is not true for what we mean by "governing authority."[†] The word "state" has acquired a broader meaning today and now refers not only to the "sword-function" itself, but also to the whole administrative structure that carries out this function, and then also to other functions of the same structure. Not everything that we mean by the modern word "state" can be termed "pagan" in the way the "violence of the sword"

---

[*] German *Staat.*
[†] German "Obrigkeit."

can. So we cannot exclude Christians today from actively working within the "state" understood in this broader sense. But the violence of the sword itself has not changed by virtue of the fact that those who administer the sword are also involved in administering other things. Or if things have significantly changed, that change is for the worse. For the things that are socially beneficial become jeopardized to the extent that they are bound up with the violence carried out by the state. The welfare program can, especially in times of war, be forced to support the population policy of a totalitarian state; the school system can become a propaganda machine, and the registry office can become a means of persecuting Jews. Even public services in which Christians might well find an appropriate place can become poisoned in this sense.

6. It is offensive to moderns not to measure everyone by the same standard. Representative of this viewpoint is the philosopher Immanuel Kant whose basic principle is: One can call an action good only if one can claim all people should act similarly. This stance has become the common property of all modern thinking. Everything that does not line up with this claim is critiqued as a "double standard." And yet this stance is neither Christian, nor is it realistic. Christians are able to follow Jesus only because they have experienced forgiveness and can depend on the power of the Holy Spirit. People for whom these preconditions are not met cannot possibly be disciples of Jesus on their own account. It would be utopian to expect a Christian life from them, and unloving and legalistic to demand it. And yet a Christian is both expected and required to live a Christian life. If one wants to call that a "double standard," so be it. It is, however, the only stance which takes faith seriously as the basic condition of Christian behavior. It is therefore a logical error when those who refuse military service today are continually confronted with the reproach already brought against the

Anabaptists in the sixteenth century and the Christians in the second century: "If everyone were to behave as you do, the state itself would go under." However self-evident this might seem to moderns, there is a logical mistake here, for to assume that everyone would behave as Christians corresponds neither to Christian faith itself, nor to reality. People are in fact not all the same. To require the same from everyone, whether or not they are believers, would be the highest form of injustice.

7. The last supposed change in situation for the church we know today concerns the general right to vote and democracy itself as a form of statehood. Since all citizens, and that includes Christians, have the right to vote and also take advantage of it, all become responsible for the state. One can no longer ask whether we *want* to participate; the citizens *are* the state. This way of thinking is also less self-evident than people might suppose. There is no absolute difference, only a relative difference, between a democracy and other forms of statehood. It is not clear that in places where there is no general right to vote, the people have no way at all of influencing the state leaders. Nor can it be proven that citizens who have the right to vote can always truly influence state leaders. According to this theory the voter *is* the state; but if so, the voter is the state in quite a different way than the state official, the jailor, and the soldier are. Citizens have a (very weak) influence on how violence is *regulated*, but they are not among those who *carry it out*. This difference is not to be ignored. According to this theory, the apostle Paul was the Roman state, an odd inference, showing that this way of thinking is not all that convincing. But even if it were convincing, it would only apply to those voters who do in fact vote along with the majority. Those who have explicitly voted against the decisions of the majority can hardly be said to be responsible for the decisions made on the basis of their right to vote.

With these comments we do not intend to present brand

new insights into a theory of the state. But it should have become clear that there is no justification for the off-handed rejection of the New Testament teaching that so often occurs when people assume the changed situation makes that teaching irrelevant for today. The Christian who takes the New Testament as norm in other aspects of faith and life has no basis for rejecting the New Testament as normative in its teaching about the state. The results of our investigation of the New Testament (i.e. the state's use of violent force is a necessary but nevertheless pagan function) remains, despite all the progress in civilization and all the changes in the current situation, just as valid as it ever was.

Several Theses

The last significant question we come to is this one: If Christians today, instead of considering the basic viewpoint of the New Testament (and of Anabaptism) out of date, would take it seriously and put it into practice, what would that look like? We can gain some guidelines from the observations made thus far, which can help us in individual situations as we attempt to discern the way of discipleship.

1. We will guard against thinking "it's all the same." The question is not *whether* we have a responsibility to the state, but *how* we fulfill our responsibility. It is not "one and the same," whether we make use of our right to vote or become a soldier. It is not "all the same," whether a Mennonite farmer is voted into the office of mayor without any initiative on his part (as has sometimes happened), or whether one strives to get into a higher political office. This is not the same as being an official in state functions related to schools, social programs, forestry and transportation, or for that matter paying taxes. Participation by Christians in one aspect of the state does not obligate the Christian in any way to participate in another one.

2. We will assume that the basic lines of the New

Testament's teaching concerning the state continue to be valid for that aspect of the state which involves the violence of the sword. Other areas of service within the state will be evaluated in part by the extent to which they are linked to this function of the state.

3. We will remember, along with the New Testament church, that one form of political responsibility is to refuse, under certain circumstances, to participate in the life of the state, namely in those situations where the state oversteps the boundaries of its mandate, as in totalitarianism, and in those situations where the state's responsibilities differ from those of the Christian, as in the military.

4. We will stop believing what our school books keep telling us, namely that all history is the history of states. The view that the Christian church and not the state stands in the middle of God's rule over the world is not only a statement of faith; it is also historical fact. Schools and hospitals, honesty and a work ethic are achievements of Christianity; it is not the state that brought these about. Just as the church of the Middle Ages developed schools and hospitals, so also Christians today can and should be pioneers in the carrying out of ministries which the state, for lack of ideas or interest, is not well-equipped (e.g., voluntary services, nonviolent conflict resolution, humane treatment of those with mental illnesses, etc.). And if Christians have a responsibility in terms of general welfare services (which should not be left to the state alone), this is even more true with respect to the central mandate of the Christian church, "to proclaim the virtues of the One who called them into the light." In fact, in terms of its service to the state and to the general welfare, the church serves most effectively and in its own most essential and irreplaceable way when it seriously goes about the business of being Christian, proclaiming the Gospel, modeling an exemplary community life, and praying for all people. The Christian who wants to put the role of Christian living

into second place in order to serve the state as a first priority is like a musician who leaves the stage in order to work as an usher in the concert hall. Of course the usher is also necessary; but the musician cannot be replaced in his or her role. And musicians, of all people, should know that they are of most value when they perform the role that no one else can fill. If the musician is not on stage, and there is therefore no concert, then the usher's role has no meaning either.

5. The state exists for the purpose of keeping order. The more a state aspires to a higher mission, a semi-religious role or one designed to control world history, whether in the west or in the east, the more the Christian will become suspicious with respect to the state.

6. We will not give in to the view that human autonomy is given up when a person becomes part of the state machinery. We will address government officials just as we do other citizens, not treating them as mere cogs in a machine, but rather as persons who are free to oppose the machine's gears when a responsible decision requires them to do so.

7. Whether Christians are acting as responsible Christians or not when serving the common good in a government position will be determined by whether or not they are free to step out if the government position were to require actions that are not Christian.

8. We will not ask: "Is this or that action forbidden for the Christian?" That is a legalistic stance from which the Christian, in contrast to the state, has been set free. "'All things are lawful,' but not all things are helpful" (1 Cor. 10:23). Christians who take their cues from the New Testament (and from Anabaptism) will not try to determine what is forbidden, but rather will look for the greatest opportunities to serve fellow humans. They will seek vocations and positions where they will have the greatest freedom and responsibility for such service.

9. We will not assume, as virtually all Christians since Constantine have, that the world is made up of Christians

only. There are many people in the world in whose lives the basic preconditions for following Christ are absent and who are not only perfectly capable, but also eagerly willing to serve in the context of the state. It is completely irresponsible to speak as though such people do not exist, and to claim that our society would go to ruin if Christians did not help along in every area, including the military. That this is illogical has already been demonstrated with the illustration of the musician and the usher.

10. There is no justification for Christians, based on these considerations, to rest self-justified and proud of their own piety, and leave the world to ruin. On the contrary! If we were to take seriously the New Testament teaching concerning the high honor and irreplaceable assignment of the church in and for the world, as presented here, then our "light would shine before people" in a way never before imagined. Our witness, our services of love, our difference from the world and our sacrifice for the world would reveal in far greater measure whose disciples we are. The New Testament viewpoint is neither consoling nor glorifying for the contemporary church. Rather it is—and this applies also to us Mennonites, *especially* to us Mennonites, who want to be seen as heirs of our ancestors in the faith—a message of judgment, a call to repentance, and a challenge to renewal.

For us moderns, accustomed as we are to rationalistic and non-Christian[*] thinking, the present attempt to understand and submit to the New Testament teaching about the state seems audacious, proud and repulsive. The high esteem for the church of Christ and the church's stance toward the state that follows from it, as these have been established from Scripture, are no less offensive and foreign to the natural sensitivities of the author of these lines than to those of the readers. And yet, could it not be that the cause of the current

---

[*] German *heidnisch*.

crisis in Christendom and the Christian West is that we today, just as in the Middle Ages, as heirs of the Anabaptist tradition, just as in the territorial churches, have not believed this saving offensive Gospel? The message of the cross is always a scandal for those who are seeking power, foolishness for those who want wisdom; "But to those who are called, . . . the power of God and the wisdom of God" (1 Cor. 1:24). If we were to believe in this power and wisdom of God, we would not see in the New Testament teaching concerning the state a backwards legalism, nor a pietistic escape from the world, nor an irresponsible anachronism. Rather we would see the gospel, the freeing, authoritative, good news of God in Christ. "For God's foolishness is wiser than human wisdom, and God's weakness is stronger than human strength" (1 Cor. 1:25).

— II —

Following Christ as a Form of Political Responsibility

The Problem

Around 1950 an old question [i.e. concerning the Christian's relationship to military action] surfaced in Germany as the country began again to arm itself. Very quickly, especially among Protestants, two basically different answers crystallized. Both were based, as one might expect for Protestants in Germany, on an interpretation of answers found in the time of the Reformation.

For the one group, in which there were many "nuclear pacifists," the basis of a social ethic is the "imperative of the hour" which emerges "out of the middle of life." This is determined in each unique situation by prophetic insight and by conscience. The basis for this appeal to the "situation" is the Reformation concept of God's ever-living Word, and the fear of fixed and impersonal "principles" that follows from this. The conscience, which here takes the place of the law, is responsible to no one. It is free. In this way many Christians came to a sort of "practical pacifism," one not founded on any universal judgment, but rather one that took it to be self-evident, given the reality of the "hour," that in an atomic age weapons are no longer permitted. However, this "conscience" (or for that matter the claim to have heard a specific guidance out the "situation") cannot be explained further.

The other "classic" solution considers the social ethic of Luther to be valid even for today. What was called "war" in the sixteenth century and that for which we are being armed today are essentially the same. What Luther called "government officials"* is not all that different from the contemporary administrative state. So we need only to repeat the claims that were made then. Just as the normal citizens of that day were simply supposed to obey and had no right to imagine they were capable of judging whether a war was just or unjust, so too we should leave the tasks of politics to political experts. Those who are called into military service should follow this call as God's cue.

The representatives of both groups have, in the past years, talked past each other so long that they are tired of talking, though they have not really listened. And no great clarity has emerged through the fact that they both based their views (and in my opinion anachronistically) on the sixteenth century. Neither dialogue nor a clear proclamation of God's command for today have emerged. Along this track, no one makes any progress. The necessary word will not be found by basing our search on the sixteenth century. The sixteenth century did not satisfactorily solve the problem; rather it raised the problem. In what follows we want to examine the New Testament to find an answer. Our goal in doing so is not to present any new insights. We simply want to examine a series of well-known fundamental ideas in the light of a new way of posing the question.

The viewpoint, in itself not a specifically Christian view-

---

* German: *Obrigkeit.*

point, that the human person in some way corresponds to God, is widely represented already in the Old Testament. The claim that the human person has been created "in the image of God" (however one understand this) means at minimum that the human person, in what he/she is and does, corresponds to God's own being. This fact of being in God's image is never debated; it is neither preached nor impressed on people; it is simply assumed. The basis of the Sabbath command through a reference to God resting at the completion of creation (Exod. 20) or its basis on the humane-ness of God, expressed in the freeing of the enslaved Israelites from Egypt (Exod. 3), makes sense only when we take into account the correspondence between God and humanity. "Be holy, for I am holy" (Lev. 11:44) may well have been a cultic rather than an ethical commandment at first; nevertheless, a tradition of "following God" attached itself to this command throughout the prophetic tradition and through Judaism right up to Martin Buber.

What the Old Testament assumed as a fundamental concept becomes a new reality in the New Testament with the pouring out of the Holy Spirit. "Child of God," "transformed into the image of Christ," "participation in the resurrection," and "in Christ" are expressions describing this new relationship to God, or rather to Christ, and make clear why the Christian is to be no different and to act no different than Christ, a member of whose body the Christian has become. It should be a self-evident implication of this that we should follow Jesus and act as he did with respect to Christ's relationship to evil, just as we do in other matters. This is the viewpoint that is represented, for example, by G. McGregor.[1] Yet the fact that we express this basic claim about which one can speak so edifyingly does not in any way deal with the real need; it merely reveals to us what our need is. The disunity, or for that matter helplessness, of Christians with respect to politics sets in right here. A majority of theologians agree with this general claim, but do not allow it to cast any light on the matter of politics. That we are to love the evildoers in the same way God loves them is accepted by these theologians in general; accepted, that is, in the family circle and in other areas of life, but not in terms of the state. That is why it will not suffice to speak about discipleship in general; rather the question needs to be asked in a much narrower and more difficult form: Does the command to follow Jesus apply for the Christian also in the realm of politics?

Our first question concerns what it would mean if the answer were "no." If one were to claim that Jesus Christ, the person who lived around the year 30, cannot be our standard, then it would follow that there must be other standards that do apply. But what do we mean when we speak of *other* standards? For Helmut Gollwitzer the other standards are somehow present in the situation, though one's dialogue partner who evaluates the situation differently cannot recognize which rules apply when the conscience interprets the situation. For professor Künneth these guiding principles are imbedded in the creation order, even though we do not know: a) whether this order represents the pure good creation of God (how then can it give us the right to kill?) or the fallen creation (how then can it still be our authority?); nor [do we know], b) by what rules we can reliably and clearly recognize these principles. Reinhold Niebuhr declares that the human Jesus is of no relevance for the content of our ethics, since Jesus as a truly prophetic spirit never intended to provide a social ethic; as a result our national life needs to be determined from pagan notions of justice, which we get from the Greco-Roman tradition.

Niebuhr is to be given a great deal of credit for admitting the non-Christian[*] character of this approach. It is indeed non-Christian[†] if we allow *other guidelines* to be valid

---

[*] German *heidnischen*.
[†] German *heidnisch*.

alongside Jesus Christ. The issue here is not pacifism, but rather the basic issue of confessing Christ. Shall we really concede that in the matter of social ethics, especially with reference to the state, it is not valid (as it is in other matters) to confess Jesus Christ—and here the human Palestinian Jesus of Nazareth is meant—as the only Word of God? Neither Gollwitzer nor Künneth, not to mention the church father, Luther, whom both claim as their basis, would have conceded this as calmly as Niebuhr does. Yet have they not clearly revealed how it can be avoided by the use of terms like "conscience" and "order"? That each one is distancing himself from the fanaticism that each sees embodied in the stance of the other does not provide the desired backing either. Our concern is not to prescribe how these various approaches should act responsibly in the world; our concern is to observe in their mutual talking past each other where each person stands, and who is not prepared to reason from the perspective of discipleship. The one who does not stand on the rock which is Christ has nothing more to say. One chooses a philosophy of order, the other a philosophy of conscience, the third a philosophy of necessary compromises, and no one can convince the others.

Jesus Christ as a Political Person

It should have become obvious in his sketchy critique of Protestant state-theologies which thesis we intend to present. We claim to have heard the New Testament say that revelation is to be found in Jesus Christ, and we do not understand why this should not apply also with reference to the state. We do not find this revelation in some sort of theory of history that is oriented toward Christ, but rather in the person from Nazareth who we confess was truly God's Son. That means revelation is not to be found in Jesus only because he participated in creation as the Logos (Word), not only because through the incarnation he "took upon himself" the world in its distress, not only because justification through his death has freed us to act responsibly, or because the resurrection represents an affirmation of life, or because his ascension has made him Lord of the world. As essential as these basic convictions are, none of them help to solve our problem. They are abstract concepts which are correct and useful, but which do not yet tell us how we are to act in the world. As general concepts, they need to be filled with the historicity of Jesus Christ.

The approach we must learn from Christ in terms of our political responsibilities derives not only from his instruction, such as the Sermon on the Mount. Jesus' instruction in the Sermon on the Mount is indeed already more concrete than these abstract concepts. Here some very clear statements are made. Here we are explicitly told how a believer is to act in specific situations. And yet it is still debatable how this instruction is intended. The order-theologian reads them quite differently than the conscience-theologian. We are therefore forced to formulate our thesis even more clearly, to work it out even more narrowly in terms of historicity.

The political existence of the incarnate one, that is the decisions of Jesus in the face of his political problems, are a revelation of God's command in the realm of politics.

The first question, then, is the question of whether Jesus was a political person at all. A perspective that is widely held today clearly answers by saying that he was self-evidently not. The claim is that he lived in circumstances completely different than our own. In the little region of Galilee where he was active, the problems we face today did not even exist. New Testament exegetes are conspicuously of the opposite opinion (and even one who is not a New Testament exegete would surely want to ask if Galilee was not similar to a contemporary rebellious colonial region). In the viewpoint of the

well-known New Testament scholar, C. H. Dodd, Jesus was
faced with all the political problems we come in contact with
today. It pays, therefore, to get to know Jesus in terms of his
political dimensions.[2]

In the temptations Jesus faced after his baptism we
encounter the question as to the meaning and direction of his
work. The offer of world rulership (the third temptation in
Matthew's order) is not the only temptation that had a political meaning. When the devil proposed that Jesus throw himself down from the pinnacle of the temple, he did not mean
that Jesus should show the people through an acrobatic stunt
what sort of tricks he could perform. Rather, we need to
imagine what it would have looked like had Jesus come
plunging down from heaven into the court of the temple.
"And the Lord whom you seek will suddenly come to his
temple" (Mal. 3:1). That would have been the most obvious
way to proceed if he had wanted to present himself suddenly
as the Messiah whom the people expected. Also, in terms of
the first temptation of Jesus, we may ask whether the sum-
mons to create bread was only about satisfying his personal
hunger. At least we can propose as a serious hypothesis the
question: Was it not a temptation for Jesus to pave the way
for the coming kingdom by solving his people's bread problem? That would bring even more clarity to the implications
of the bread miracle in the time of his public ministry, which
Maurice Goguel characterizes as the "Galilean Crisis." This
crisis represented both the high point and the breaking off of
the Galilean activity of the Lord. His miracle-working and
his teaching ministry reached their pinnacle in the bread miracle. The people who had come running after him in ever-
increasing numbers believed that the decisive moment had
come and wanted to make Jesus their king, that is the leader
of a rebellion. Jesus had produced bread, somewhat in the
way the devil had proposed, and now he was faced with the
political consequences of his deed. Now he would be able to

reestablish the kingdom of Israel. But he did not take the road that stood there temptingly before him. He withdrew, and from that point on engaged himself primarily with his small circle of disciples. Now for the first time, he revealed his glory on the Mount of Transfiguration. At this point he explained to his disciples that he had to suffer and die. Precisely now "he set his face toward Jerusalem."

The week of the final decision begins with a large-scale political demonstration: the triumphal entry into Jerusalem. In the events the church celebrates on Palm Sunday, the uniqueness of our Lord's political stance becomes especially visible. On one side we see Jesus still faced with a temptation, with a choice of an essentially political nature. He is greeted by the cheering crowds as the coming Son of David. He appears in the temple, claiming an authority that cannot be evaluated as anything but messianic, before which the people fall back in unexplainable fear, even though he stands alone and without weapons (unless one believes that the temple police and the Roman guard are afraid of his whip). Now the time has come. "The Lord, whom you seek will suddenly come to his temple . . . he will purify the sons of Levi" (Mal. 3:1, 3). And yet, in the face of this opportunity, Jesus decides just as he had previously done. He rides on a donkey, a decidedly un-kingly animal according to Jewish notions of the day. He weeps for the city that is not willing for him to gather its children. In the temple, where the situation is fully ripe for a political coup, he lets the opportunity slip by and withdraws to Bethany.[3] No wonder the Zealots and the crowd are disappointed and soon find themselves ready to swap Jesus for the Zealot leader Barabbas.

But with this the political temptation is not yet over. What was his prayer all about when, in the night of temptation, he prayed, "If it be possible, let this cup pass from me" (Matt. 26:39). What would it have meant for him to want the cup to pass from him? What would have enabled him to sidestep the cross? "Edifying exegesis" has hardly ever asked the question. For "political exegesis" this question is central. How could he have avoided the cross? We do not know in detail what other way of acting he considered in that hour. But we can hardly be wrong in assuming it would have required a holy war. We read of the legions of angels that Jesus claimed he could have called on, and of the sword Peter had ready for legitimate defense and also used. It is not a new assumption that Judas, by betraying Jesus, was not intending to hand him over; rather he thought he could in this way force Jesus to save himself and finally usher in the war out of which Judas the "Sicarii" (Zealot) hoped the Kingdom of God would break through.

We see that Jesus was, from beginning to end, a political person. Not only his sermon concerning God's Reign/ Kingdom (was there any more politically colored word he could have chosen than that?) but also his deeds were of highest political relevance. One of the options he could have chosen was to carry out his program by means of violent revolution, supported both by the Zealots and his own miracle-working power. But precisely because this was not God's will, Jesus rejected this option and was crucified for doing so. The inscription above the cross indicated the legal grounds for his execution: he was the "King of the Jews." At the same time both highly political in his kingdom message and also to outward appearances non-political in his rejection of the most readily available political means of setting up his kingdom, he died (just as we die today) because people were not willing to recognize (as we also do not want to recognize) that "political" does not always mean "governmental."

Before we proceed, a common objection should be mentioned. People often attempt to wipe out the ethical meaning of Jesus' final acts; after all, he "had to die." Above all Anselm of Canterbury (1033-1109) presented the matter like this: An innocent, incarnate, divine being had to die in order to bring salvation to the world. If Jesus pushed aside the crown, he did so (according to Anselm) not as the morally right thing to do, but only in order to be able to die. In response one can ask right up front why Jesus had to die in this way. If it was simply a matter of an incarnate divine being having to die, he could have died much more easily, for example when Herod killed the babies in Bethlehem, or perhaps in a traffic accident. There is a deeper issue here, however. We misunderstand the relationship between Christ's two natures if we wipe out the political side of his human existence. If one does not view the political decisions of Jesus as truly human political decisions, as is the case with the objection mentioned above, we label that Docetism (denial of the true humanity of Christ). One can also recognize these decisions as real and genuine, but then deny them any revelational quality. Dogmatic theology calls that Ebionism (denial of the true divinity of Christ). According to the New Testament, Jesus' death was not some kind of metaphysical experience in itself, as some theories of atonement claim; rather it was a perfect ethical act, the highpoint of Christ's obedience (Heb. 5:8ff.; Phil. 2).

The Cross of Christians as Political Discipleship

It is the consistent assumption of the New Testament that Jesus lives on in the church, Christ's body, and that this becomes visible where the church follows Jesus in innocent suffering.

"If any one comes to me and does not hate his own father and mother and wife and children and brothers and sisters, yes, and even his own life, he cannot be my disciple" (Luke 14:26).

"The cup that I drink you will drink; and with the baptism with which I am baptized, you will be baptized" (Mark 10:39).

"If the world hates you, know that it has hated me before it hated you . . . 'A servants is not greater than his master.' If they persecuted me, they will persecute you" (John 15:18-20).

"Always carrying in the body the death of Jesus, so that the life of Jesus may also be manifested in our bodies" (2 Cor. 4:10).

"That I may know him and the power of his resurrection, and may share his sufferings, becoming like him in his death" (Phil. 3:10).

"In my flesh I complete what is lacking in Christ's afflictions" (Col. 1:24).

Though Paul is speaking about himself in these last texts, the same applies to the church:

"For it has been granted to you that for the sake of Christ you should not only believe in him but also suffer for his sake . . . Have this mind among yourselves, which is yours in Christ Jesus" (better translated: ". . . that is appropriate for those in Christ Jesus.") (Phil. 1:29, 2:5).

"Indeed all who desire to live a godly life in Christ Jesus will be persecuted" (2 Tim. 3:12).

What this means is that the cross of the church is a continuation of the cross of Christ, just as the church itself is his body which lives on.

"But if when you do right and suffer for it you take it patiently, you have God's approval. For to this you have been called, because Christ also suffered for you, leaving you an example, that you should follow in his steps" (1 Pet. 2:20-21).

"By this we know love, that he laid down his life for us; and we ought to lay down our lives for the brethren" (1 John 3:16).

"As he is so are we in this world" (1 John 4:17).[4]

That is how the heart of the early church speaks without even being asked, even when the flow of thought does not require such statements. This is not a particularly Pauline, or Petrine, or Johannine viewpoint; it is simply the common property of the early church. Christ lives in us; the life which we now live in the flesh—it is not we who live it, but Christ who is in us (Gal. 2:20).

To speak of the cross of the Christian or of the church is commonplace in ordinary pious language. These are talked about a great deal, especially in pastoral care. But if we have established that the cross of Christ was a highly political experience, then the cross of the church must also be understood in a new light. In pastoral counseling the language of the cross is readily used to help people find strength to deal with their rheumatism or to get along with an annoying mother-in-law. But that is not what the cross is about; at least that is not its primary meaning.

Jesus' cross was not some unexplainable and undeserved evil that came upon him accidentally, like a disease, a storm, or an earthquake. No matter how much love we have, and want to demonstrate, for victims of disease and accident, the issue for Jesus was not some inescapable suffering. On the contrary, Jesus' cross was a form of suffering that Jesus could very well have avoided. It was the cost of his obedience in the midst of a rebellious world. It will be no different for us. The early church was not in a position to decide whether or not they would take over the Roman Empire.[*] They were and they remained a persecuted minority. From that perspective one could explain their stance in relation to the state as a solution arrived at by default. But that is not what it was. The way of suffering which they had no choice but to follow was never viewed as some misfortune that really should not have happened; on the contrary, they viewed it as completely normal, as appropriate, as that which was fitting, given the essential character of the state and of the church. It would be a misunderstanding if we viewed the early church's teaching about the state as if it were the result of some dis-

---

[*] German *Staat*.

appointment. That would be to forget the essential connection between Christ and his church.

But now we must ward off the most serious misunderstanding of all. The essence of following Jesus is not grasped if we view it primarily as a commandment to become the same as Jesus, or to act the way Jesus did; rather following Jesus really means basing our action on our participation in Christ's very being. That is why those who criticize the whole notion of "following Jesus," and who try to make it look ridiculous by asking whether we should not also copy Jesus' singleness, his occupation as a carpenter, or his habit of walking barefoot, have missed the point altogether. This is not about some legalistic approach to copying Jesus, but rather about participating in Christ. We are already part of his body; we do not become so through following him. Following Jesus is the result, not the means, of our fellowship with Christ. It is the form of our Christian freedom and not a new law.

The Separation of the Cross and the Sword

We began by observing that many theologians recognize in a general sense the concept of following Jesus; they do not, however, accept it as applicable for the realm of politics. Now we have seen that there is no justification in the New Testament for limiting the scope of its validity in this way. Nevertheless, the problem that such theologians hope to solve by the limitation they make still needs to be addressed. What should we expect from the state? Do we expect cross-carrying followership? Or do we simply write off the state, since the state neither can nor wants to adopt that standard? Actually this question does not directly relate to our topic, but it is so pervasively present in the background that we must touch on it.

It was self-evident in the time of the New Testament that the state was pagan. Can God still use a pagan state? If Christians would not take seriously their responsibility to be involved in the affairs of state, would the state not slip out of God's control?

We are well aware of the Old Testament witness that God directs the affairs of all nations. The Assyrians are called "the rod of God's wrath." Nebuchadnezzar was ascribed the title "Servant of God," and Israel was to give up its own statehood to him. The emperor Cyrus was even called—how awful—"Messiah," "my servant," "the one whom God loves." Isaiah 45 responds to the feuding of the Jews, who did not want to let God make use of pagan kings in this way. The New Testament makes very clear that the state is simultaneously outside the church and yet within Christ's dominion, pagan and yet still in God's hand. Both the state and the church are directed by God, but in very different ways. The state represents human activity outside of faith; through its sword God acts. The church is the form of human action within the context of faith; through its cross God acts as well. Only the Christian cannot do both of them at the same time, as God can. The state is there for the sake of the church and not vice versa.

No doubt modern sensibilities view it as impudent and presumptuous for the church of the new covenant to cherish such a conception of its own importance. And of course those who wish are free to reject this view and keep on believing that the meaning of history is carried by the progress of the western way of life (or the eastern for that matter). Only those who do so need to know what they are throwing away, namely the basic thought pattern of the whole New Testament, participation "in Christ," and the confession "Jesus is Lord."

It is remarkable how the meaning of Christ's lordship has been reversed in modern ecumenical discussion. In New Testament times the lordship of Christ meant that even that which is pagan, the state, was under God's rule. Today exactly the same expression means that Christians have been sent into all areas of public life, including every political position, and that there as Christians they are to do their duties according to the rules of the state—in other words, the opposite of the meaning in the New Testament. Back then the concept of Christ's Lordship served to explain why the Christian should live as a follower of Jesus and not try to make the state Christian; now it is used to explain why the Christian, in order to work in the government, must live by standards foreign to the Christian way. This reversal is significant. The fact that it is done without further thought indicates how hard it is for western Christianity to look back beyond Augustine and Constantine all the way to the thought world of the New Testament, or for that matter to look across the ocean and see the real situation of Christianity in the non-Western world.

Still there are signs of hope that we might yet be able to think about the state (that is about the administration of the sword) as the early church did. Many recent experiences have demonstrated clearly that the state does not intend to be merely a rational non-ideological administrative instrument within Christendom, as classical Lutheranism required and assumed; rather the state itself wants to become a religion. One has been able to hear this desire in the "Christian west" in claims like this: The church cannot forbid the state to be ready to defend itself, but must nevertheless tell individual Christians that it would be a sin to participate in military service. Whether or not this is correct is not the issue here. What we want to take note of here is that it represents a way of thinking about the state which does not expect the state to be "in the faith."

Discipleship Today

The contemporary meaning of what we have established from the New Testament is self-evidently dependent on the decision we make—partly a faith decision and partly a methodological one—as to whether and how we will allow the New Testament to apply today. We will not be able to unpack all aspects of this problem here. Nor will it be possible to present examples showing what it would look like if we were to accept the witness of Scripture as God's Word and would respect the non-Christian* character of the state's use of the sword while also proclaiming Christ's lordship over the state. We will attempt no more than to explain the basic decisions that have to be considered here.

The perspective that the New Testament teaching applies also today is opposed by two other perspectives. Both take the position that we can no longer view the state's use of the sword as a form of un-faith. But they reach this conclusion in two quite opposite ways and we cannot simultaneously carry on a conversation with both of them, insincerely putting forward arguments from both sides at the same time. On the one hand, one can simply deny that the New Testament view is as indicated above, and then attempt to discern a New Testament view in John the Baptist's message to the soldiers (Luke 3:14) or in texts like Luke 14:31.

On the other hand, one can admit that the New Testament does indeed think about the sword as we claim, but then go on to claim that this view is wrong, or at least no longer correct: wrong, because the return of Christ did not occur as anticipated and it was necessary to come to terms with the world; or no longer correct, because a change set in with Constantine and the Christianizing of the rulers, or with the Enlightenment and the responsibility of the individual person for the democratic state, a change that has essentially transformed the world and with it also the role of the sword. A continuing dialogue with the first of these positions would involve basic exegetical work; with the second one would have to address the problem from a dogmatic perspective.

We cannot deny that the state today looks very different

---

* German *heidnischen.*

than it did in the first century. In claiming the New Testament teaching applies today we do not want to dispute at all that massive changes have taken place. The question is rather how we should respond to the new and different situation. Here, too, we have to distinguish between two problem areas that are often run together.

On the one hand, the administrative instrument we call the "state" today does its work in many respects quite differently than it once did. With the right to vote, the state's subjects have more opportunity to influence both the participants in and the stance of the government. Furthermore, the modern state takes on tasks that have little or nothing to do with the exercise of the sword. These innovations provide a challenge for Christian ethics, especially if the New Testament is to provide guidance (if it is not to provide guidance then there is no problem; the innovations are simply accepted as they come).

The changes, however, do not change the essence of the "sword." The military aspect of the state does not become Christian just because the state also builds hospitals and schools. It will be necessary to find a whole variety of ways of applying the New Testament perspective to these other functions of the state and the Christian will be able to carry out ministries in many positions we could call "governmental" (belonging to the state). Nevertheless, what the Scriptures teach about the administration of the sword remains basically untouched by these changes.

On the other hand, with the so-called Constantinian-Augustinian turnaround, the princes and thereby the whole western world has become Christian. And that has been evaluated by the Middle Ages and by the Reformation as a giant step forward, sometimes even as an eschatological turning-point. The Swiss reformer Heinrich Bullinger summarized the Reformation view when he said that the princes had become "saviors and nourishers" of the church. The administration of the sword is no longer the work of pagans, those who are not believers but whom God still uses for divine purposes, nor is the use of the sword considered a necessary evil within Christendom; rather (according to the Reformers), it is the most distinguished of all professions. The Reformation even outdid the Middle Ages when the church itself exercised authority through the agency of the territorial government. Reformers surpassed the Middle Ages further in their teaching about the invisibility of the true church, taught in order to make this reversal of the relationship between the church and world tolerable. Here we can only conclude that this is not a legitimate application of the New Testament's teaching about the sword; it is a sacrifice of it. Whether this surrender is a good thing or not, we need not further address. The decision as to whether or not the Scriptures should be considered valid is one that people cannot make for each other.

For now it will have to suffice to establish that a clear dialogue depends on distinguishing between taking the early Christian position seriously and giving up that position. And we will have to be clear that we cannot simply cover up the differences with the slogan, "the world has changed."

Notes

I. The State in the New Testament

1. Editor's Note: In Yoder's presentation he was not making the distinction that is often made today in historical or exegetical literature between the "early church" (i.e. the very earliest church in Jerusalem) and other terms sometimes used to refer to the church described in Acts, the letters and the first three centuries.

II. Following Christ as a Form of Political Responsibility

1. G. McGregor, *Der Friede auf Erden*, (München, 1955).

2. As far as I can tell, I am not presenting any new exegetical insights, but simply the consensus of the research. Additional comments are found in Oscar Cullmann, *The State in the New Testament*, (New York, 1956); Maurice Goguel, *The Life of Jesus,* (New York, 1949), especially the chapter on the Galilean Crisis; Vincent Taylor, *The Ministry of Jesus*, (London, 1955).

3. Here we are viewing the entry into Jerusalem and the cleansing of the temple as consecutive events, as presented in Matthew and Luke. The matter does not change in any important respect if (as in Mark) a night separated the two events.

4. We are omitting the material in Heb. 11 and 12 only because of its length. The relationship between the suffering of Christ (12:1ff.), the suffering of the witnesses (ch. 11), and that of believers (12:3ff.) is clearly the same as we find in these other texts.

The Author

John Howard Yoder (1927-1997) taught ethics and theology as a professor at Notre Dame University and Associated Mennonite Biblical Seminary. He received his doctorate from the University of Basel, Switzerland, and was a member of the Mennonite Church in Elkhart, Indiana. Widely sought around the world as a theological educator, ethicist, and interpreter of biblical pacifism, he is best known for his study on *The Politics of Jesus*.

The Translator

Timothy J. Geddert teaches New Testament at Mennonite Brethren Biblical Seminary in Fresno, California, and is author of *Mark*, a volume in the Believers Church Bible Commentary Series. Tim is married to Gertrud Andres and they have spent several extended periods of time living and ministering in Germany.